OB
G
WORD

OBEYING GOD'S WORD

CHRISTIAN CLASSICS SERIES

The call to true discipleship

by
Alan M. Stibbs

Inter-Varsity Press

INTER-VARSITY PRESS
38 De Montfort Street, Leicester LE1 7GP, England

First published 1955
First published in Christian Classics, 1996

British Library Cataloguing in Publication Data
A catalogue record for this book is available from the British Library.

ISBN 0-85111-241-2

Printed and bound in Great Britain by Cox & Wyman Ltd, Reading, Berkshire.

Inter-Varsity Press is the book-publishing division of the Universities and Colleges Christian Fellowship (formerly the Inter-Varsity Fellowship), a student movement linking Christian Unions in universities and colleges throughout the United Kingdom and the Republic of Ireland, and a member movement of the International Fellowship of Evangelical Students. For information about local and national activities write to UCCF, 38 De Montfort Street, Leicester LE1 7GP.

CONTENTS

		PAGE
	PREFACE	7
I.	THE IMPORTANCE OF OBEDIENCE	9
II.	TEMPTATION AND DEFEAT	15
III.	TEMPTATION AND VICTORY	21
IV.	OBEYING THE GOSPEL	28
V.	TRUE DISCIPLESHIP	37
VI.	PERILS IN THE WAY	43
VII.	THE PRACTICE OF OBEDIENCE (1)	49
VIII.	THE PRACTICE OF OBEDIENCE (2)	63
IX.	THE ULTIMATE ISSUES	73

PREFACE

THERE is a tendency today for students of the Bible to be too exclusively intellectual and theoretical in their approach, too detached, too absorbed in the scientific investigation of how the Scriptures were written, and what they meant to their first writers and readers. The danger is lest we grow only in critical knowledge of the Bible, instead of, through its use, growing in knowledge of God and in obedience to His will. For, as a divinely provided handbook for the use of His people, it is intended by God to promote knowledge of Him, understanding of His ways, enjoyment of His grace and salvation, and active co-operation in the doing of His will. The practical demands which the Bible makes on its readers are, therefore, spiritual and moral. It invites the Godward response of faith and obedience, of reverence and right living. We need, therefore, pointedly to ask ourselves whether we have adequately faced up in this way to the practical authority of the Word of God as that which should determine what we believe, what we teach, and how we act. The simple purpose of this book is to use the witness and exposition of the Scriptures themselves to press home this challenge.

ALAN M. STIBBS.

IMPORTANT NOTE: *Those who would read this book with full understanding and profit must do so alongside an open Bible, to which they continually refer in order to read or consult the many passages mentioned and expounded.*

CHAPTER I

THE IMPORTANCE OF OBEDIENCE

I. THE IMPLICATIONS OF BIBLICAL INSPIRATION

OUR acknowledgement of the divine inspiration of the Bible is of great practical importance to us as Christians because of the function which God intends that its proper use should fulfil in our lives. This function is nowhere more decisively indicated than in the words from the Old Testament (actually from Dt. viii. 3), which our Lord Himself quoted as His first answer to the temptations of the devil. He said, '*It is written, Man shall not live by bread alone, but by every word that proceedeth out of the mouth of God.*' (Mt. iv. 4; cf. Lk. iv. 4.)

Other animals live by food; that is enough for them. But man is unique. He cannot truly live by bread alone. For him life is to be found only in conscious dependence on God, and in sustained devotion to God. It is to inspire and to inform these essential activities that the God-inspired Word has been given.

The written Word of God is thus of direct practical value for human living for two main reasons. First, it tells us what God is doing, or is willing to do. It reveals His purposes. It is a book of prophecies and promises. Second, it tells us what we ought to do in order to please God, and to share in the benefits of His activity; it also warns us what not to do if we are to avoid wrongdoing and escape God's condemnation. It is a book both of precepts and of actual or virtual prohibitions.

The true way to enjoy life is to trust and obey; on the one

hand, to count wholly on God's doing, and, on the other hand, to contribute one's own doing. Guidance for practising such a twofold response to God is to be found in the Bible. It is for the Christian the one authoritative text-book of faith and conduct.

From the Bible, then, as a handbook of the faith, we may learn what God is like, and what He has done; we may learn about the Saviour whom He sent, and gain informed conviction concerning His Person and His work; we may learn how His salvation can be made ours, and worked out in our daily lives by the indwelling Spirit; and we may learn how all these purposes of God's saving grace are to be consummated in the great coming day of the Lord, when the Saviour will re-appear and gather around Him His glorified people. All this and more of God's revealed truth we ought to know, believe, embrace and propagate. Nor can we fully enjoy and declare our faith and hope as Christians except by a detailed knowledge and understanding of all that the Bible teaches. So we ought to be diligent and prayerful students of God's Word.

The Bible is also a handbook of conduct. By its aid and instruction we are meant to learn moral discernment and thus to have our senses exercised to discern between good and evil, so that we may actively choose the good and refuse the evil. If, therefore, we are to order our lives as we ought as children of God, we need continually to put ourselves under the instruction and correction of God's written Word, and thus to let our wrong actions be exposed and condemned, and our right actions determined and approved, by its plain and pointed precepts, and by the application of its principles.

Christ commissioned His followers not only to preach the gospel, which men had only to believe in order to be saved, but also to teach converts to observe all the things which He had commanded. This is still our plain Christian obligation. Nor can we thus lead others into truths which we do not ourselves both believe and practise. Properly to live the Christian life demands, therefore, daily and detailed attention to what the Bible says. It demands not only a spirit of faith in God's promises, but also a sensitive conscience about obeying His precepts. Indeed, there is in the New Testament explicit warning that those who think they can hold fast to the faith without such conscientious obedience will make spiritual shipwreck.

We rightly acknowledge the Bible to be God's own inspired Word, because we believe that such assent is indispensable to true spiritual well-being. But soundness in the faith will not be preserved or fully guaranteed simply by signing a doctrinal basis, important as that is. For to be 'sound' in the faith means to be healthy or spiritually fit as a Christian believer. Such health is morally conditioned. We must be doers of the Word and not believers only. So we ought, by our diligent and prayerful daily study of the Bible, first to let our faith be inspired and informed, and then to let our conduct be tested and directed, by the plain and detailed teaching of God's written Word. For this is the only way properly to confirm our confession of the divine inspiration of the Bible—by consistent and conscientious use of it as our rule of faith and conduct.

II. EXPOSITION OF PSALM CXIX. 1–24, 33–35

It may be wise to confirm these general statements by some detailed exposition of an actual Bible passage. Such a passage, one obviously directly relevant to our subject, is Ps. cxix. It is of this Psalm that John Ruskin wrote that it 'has become of all the most precious to me in its overflowing and glorious passion of love for the law of God'. To appreciate this Psalm one needs to have in one's own heart and life the spirit and aspirations of the psalmist. Since this is equally true of the appreciation of the subject of this whole book, we do well to pray much for the God-given increase in us of this very spirit. The psalmist's words may serve to quicken our interest and to direct our desires in prayer. Let us look then (with a Bible open) at the first two or three stanzas of Ps. cxix.

Verses 1–8 speak of the blessedness of those who unfailingly observe God's law. The comprehensive embrace and the diverse character of God's Word are here expressed by a suggestive variety of descriptive names—His testimonies and His ways, His precepts and His statutes, His commandments and His righteous judgments or ordinances—all related to the varied circumstances and needs of human living. The practical and all-absorbing nature of man's consequent responsibility to obey—to make the only adequate response of obedience—is unmistakably indicated by such words as 'walk', 'keep' and 'do'. What is more, such response is to be made 'diligently' and 'with the whole heart' —with full concentration of mind and will. It involves having respect unto God's commandments, heeding them with the deliberate intention of acting accordingly, learning with a view to doing. This is the consuming passion of the psalmist's life. '*O that my ways were directed to keep thy statutes!*' What is thus stirred in him—and it is very important to see this clearly—is not some devotion to the impersonal law (what some would call bibliolatry), but an outgoing of spirit in worship, prayer and desire towards God Himself. Through keeping His commandments, the psalmist expects to find God, to be without shame in His presence, and to delight in His praise. So let us learn that the whole purpose of man's response to God's Word in faith and obedience is thus to realize the chief end of man, which is 'to glorify God and to enjoy Him for ever'.

Verses 9–16 indicate the way of moral purity, of keeping clean, of avoiding evil, of realizing the highest aspirations of youth. On the one hand, one must be prepared to recognize the essential character of disobedience as impurity or defilement, as wandering or turning from the divinely indicated right way to the self-willed wrong way, and, above all, as sinning against God and directly displeasing Him. On the other hand, one needs to realize how right standards of behaviour are learnt and practised by taking heed according to God's Word, by bringing one's doings daily into the light and under the judgment of the Word of God; by seeking God with one's whole heart, by being so absorbed with pleasing Him as thereby to be saved from wandering and waywardness; and by hiding God's Word in one's heart, or storing it in one's memory, so as to be able easily to recollect it and to use it to detect the beginnings of sin, and openly to delight in ways pleasing to God.

In verses 17–24 the psalmist confesses his desire for, and his delight in, the discovery and the doing of the will of God. To him the very purpose and satisfaction of life itself is to keep God's Word. His great need, his urgent prayer, is as a willing learner to understand God's law that it may illumine his darkness and inform his ignorance. This is with him an all-consuming passion, and the more so because he knows that the only alternative to this way of humility, obedience and blessing is the way of pride, error and cursing.

This urgent request for understanding with a view to obedience is particularly repeated in Ps. cxix. 33–35. Such words ought to make us all as Bible readers to examine ourselves to see whether we have the same practical end of obedience in view in all our Bible study. Also, the psalmist here teaches us by practice rather than by precept, that the beginnings of right response to this very challenge are to be found in praying as he did: '*Teach me, O Lord, the way of thy statutes; and I shall keep it unto the end. Give me understanding, and I shall keep thy law; yea, I shall observe it with my whole heart. Make me to go in the path of thy commandments; for therein do I delight.*'

CHAPTER II

TEMPTATION AND DEFEAT

THE story of the fall of man into sin is a story of man's failure to maintain practical, unquestioning obedience to the God-given Word. Let us turn to the story, as it is recorded in Gn. iii. 1–6. But first we must note that man, as a new creature in a new world, needed, and was given, some plain instructions that he might know how to act both to please God, and to promote his own well-being. What man was given was words from God—words of authority and revelation, words of objective truth and direct practical import, disclosing for man's information and benefit facts of which he would otherwise have been ignorant. '*And the Lord God commanded the man, saying, Of every tree of the garden thou mayest freely eat: But of the tree of the knowledge of good and evil, thou shalt not eat of it: for in the day that thou eatest thereof thou shalt surely die*' (Gn. ii. 16, 17). These clear directions combined both permission and prohibition. They gave both positive guidance and negative warning. They demanded and deserved unquestioning acceptance and uncompromising obedience. Man's safety depended upon their diligent observance. Man was thus challenged in his own interests to become a doer of God's Word. This was then, and still is, man's chief responsibility—to become a doer of God's Word.

Then came the devil and immediately began to seek to divert man from the pathway of obedience, and to do it by a campaign of words. He brought to the task not overpowering armaments but specious arguments. His first utterance ended with a question mark. This is how misleading propaganda commonly begins; that is, by seeking to raise doubts about things which one thought one could take for granted. Such questioning was extremely subtle; for it sought to undermine man's confidence in the one foundation on which alone he could stand secure. The one sufficient reason why Eve should have been determined to abide by the divine command was simply because God had said it. The enemy, therefore, attacked the authorship of the command as the sure way to undermine its authority. He asked, '*Hath God said?*' He raised questions such as, Are you quite sure *God* did say it? Or can He have *meant* exactly what you thought He meant? Surely it is inconceivable that a loving Creator should thus restrict the freedom of His creatures? And all the time the enemy's motive was not to promote a better understanding of the mind of God, but to persuade Eve to disown the one expression of His mind which she did possess; and thus to make herself into a creature without any authoritative guidance, and consequently one ready to be misled by cleverly designed suggestions. In other words, the enemy was out to break down her defences and to make her open to invasion by foreign ideas. His method of achieving this was the more deadly because apparently so harmless. What harm could there be in indulging in a little speculation about the trees of the garden? Yet the truth was that once Eve entertained the subject as one open to question at all, she had taken the first step towards capitulation; for she had given a treacherous foe a menacing foothold within her own mind.

Having thus obtained a foothold within Eve's mind by his questioning, the enemy at once pressed home the attack. The first stage had been to entice Eve to abandon the attitude of submissive acceptance of the divine Word, simply because it was God's Word, and to lead her to face the question on her own from her own observation of the facts. The second stage consisted in encouraging still greater presumption. The enemy now enticed Eve to adopt an attitude of superiority, to sit in judgment on the facts, to come to her own conclusion, and actually to decide against, and to reject, the Word of God, and to dare to deny or contradict it. '*Ye shall not surely die*'; surely so serious a consequence as death would not follow from the simple act of eating? The third stage completed the conquest. The enemy now invited Eve to active independence and open rebellion. He called for the full outburst of self-assertion. He appealed wholly to selfish pride. He actually suggested that the prohibition was designed to keep man out of something good, to hold him in bondage. '*For God doth know that in the day ye eat thereof, then your eyes shall be opened, and ye shall be as gods, knowing good and evil.*' One twentieth century way of putting this is that religion is dope for the masses, something that man must reject if he is ever to be free and find fulfilment. So the enemy called, as he still calls, for open rebellion, for proud presumption, for defiant ungodliness—and all by the subtlety of misleading words.

Nor was such enticement unsuccessful; Eve responded and disobeyed the divine command. Nor are similar arguments any less successful today; for it is by the same three stages that many are still deceived into departing from the Word of God. First, they depart in thought and begin to doubt the authority of the Word, then they depart in word and do not hesitate to deny the truth of the Word, and finally they depart in deed, and act in disobedience and even in deliberate defiance of the plain injunctions of the Word. All that the words of divine command can now do for man is to demonstrate that he is a sinner. '*By the law is the knowledge of sin*' (Rom. iii. 20).

There is a further question which is worthy of some detailed consideration. We have seen how the enemy advanced in his attack on Eve. '*We are,*' as St. Paul says, '*not ignorant of his devices*' (2 Cor. ii. 11). It should be no less of practical value to try to see why Eve surrendered. What from her point of view were the grounds of her decision and consequent action? What persuaded her to alter her mind and to abandon the Word of God? The answer is that there were two inducements, one from outside, the other from inside; first the enemy's suggestions, and second her own feelings and suppositions; in other words, the devil and self. She allowed these to take the place in her mind of God and His Word.

This means, in the first place, that she ceased to look up for guidance. She tried to take her bearings and to steer her course solely by local evidence, solely by the help of voices without and within, instead of by the light of God-given revelation.

What is more, it means, in the second place, that she rejected the authoritative Word of her best Friend (the Creator, who made the trees, and to whom she owed everything, i.e. the One most likely to know) for the unsupported assertion of an unknown stranger. Nor are people today any different. For this is how men are still led astray. Let us learn from Eve's mistakes to beware of approaches whose chief aim is to persuade us to abandon the best in order to follow the latest.

In the third place, Eve depended on sense observation and inner feeling. She pitted her own subjective fancy against the God-given objective fact. She used the supposed findings of natural science and psychology to oppose the plain witness of theology. God had said that to eat of this particular tree would be fatal. Eve preferred to go by her own feelings and her independent judgment. It looked pleasant. Surely such attractive-looking fruit must be good for food? In addition, the serpent said it would do her good, and that she would be the loser if she refrained from eating. So strong and irrepressible desire to eat was awakened; and this mere sensual yearning or carnal appetite won the day. Eve became a victim of misdirected instincts. Having already yielded to *ungodliness* she now yielded to *worldly lusts*. (See Tit. ii. 12.)

In the fourth place, Eve was deceived by specious rationalization—by arguments and an explanation which all seemed to justify eating. The command not to eat, because to do so would be fatal, was represented by the enemy, and slowly and surely regarded by Eve herself, as unworthy of God, unsupported by the evidence, and unfair on the creature. Consequently it was disowned as a guide to action. Eve's conscience and her innate reverence for the Word of God were overpowered and their witness silenced by the breaking down of facts and the bolstering up of fancy by specious arguments. The enemy could not of course alter the objective truth of the Word, that to eat would be fatal, but he could and did persuade Eve to alter the subjective attitude of her mind, so that she now believed that to eat would be beneficial. In other words, he persuaded her, as he still seeks to persuade men, to use reason to criticize and deny revelation, and thus to justify departure from the Word of God.

The consequence was that Eve was doubly deceived. She was enticed into choosing a false way to obtain a fancied good at the cost of forsaking the true way to avoid actual evil. Nor could she have been saved from such a fatal step except by steadfast adherence to the God-given Word. For she could herself experimentally discover whether all her theorizing about the tree was correct or not only by actually eating the fruit. And then, if her theorizing were wrong, it would be too late to avoid the consequent damage.

For example, if one found a bottle of strange liquid plainly marked 'poison', if a bystander asserted that it was not poison but a refreshing drink, and if one removed the cork and were attracted by the smell, no matter how thirsty one were, one would still, and wisely, be inclined to give the label the benefit of the doubt, and to refrain from the experiment of drinking. Too much would be at stake if one drunk, only to find that the label was right after all!

Similarly the statements of divine revelation deal with facts outside man's power to prove or disprove by logical argument. Too much is at stake for us lightly to disregard them. Even from the standpoint of prudent self-interest they deserve to be given the benefit of the doubt, in case they may be true. And when we consider their established and enduring authority, and the testimony of the thousands who have found their happiness in obeying them, it is the more obvious that our only wisdom, and indeed our only safety, is to abide by them.

It is, therefore, a tragedy of infinite gravity when misleading propaganda and presumptuous speculation cause men to their own eternal damage to disbelieve and to depart from the Word of God, and sometimes openly to deny and even to defy its plain statements and explicit commands. Yet this is where we all have failed and gone astray; leaving the way of God's commandments we have all turned to our own way. Judged by this standard of full obedience to the Word of God we all stand under condemnation and in peril of judgment as sinners.

CHAPTER III

TEMPTATION AND VICTORY

THE record of our Lord's temptations in the wilderness is remarkably complementary to the story of Gn. iii; it is its evangelical counterpart. Put together, the two stories show first, how the first Adam failed, and second, how the second Adam prevailed in the encounter with temptation. The devil first met man in the place where God had put him. Adam and Eve failed in a garden where they lacked nothing. Jesus as Man for men met the devil, by contrast, in a wilderness. He prevailed in the place where He seemed to lack everything. Success or failure, therefore, clearly does not depend on environment. Let us take the account of the temptation given us by Matthew in Mt. iv. 1–11 and consider it section by section.

(a) *Mt. iv. 1–4*

It is surely significant also that the first man's initial fall into sin and the second Man's decisive victory over temptation both involved facing an appeal to man's need of, and appetite for, food. Adam and Eve fell when they ate the fruit of the forbidden tree. Jesus prevailed when, hungry though He was, He refused to make bread to eat. Temptation, therefore, commonly has to do with appetites which in themselves are physically natural and morally neutral. What the enemy of man's soul does is to strive to exploit, to misdirect, and to degrade fundamentally proper and legitimate desires. Thus bread or food—that is, the very thing which satisfies appetite—becomes a means of enticement or testing. For, although food is a necessity of life, it is not the first necessity. It must be kept in its place as a means not an end. Man needs to recognize that there are higher interests which must be given priority even over satisfying appetite. For the ultimate guarantee of life and its continuance is found not in having food to eat, but in abiding by God's Word and in doing His will. In this pathway of obedience the servant of God is immortal till his work is done. His life will unfailingly be sustained.

So to the temptation to make bread in order to preserve life Jesus answered: '*It is written, Man shall not live by bread alone, but by every word that proceedeth out of the mouth of God.*' Indeed, to each one of the three temptations Jesus answered, *It is written;* and then quoted a plain precept or prohibition from the Scriptures. To every enticement He said in effect that there were certain things which it would be wrong to do, and that what made this absolutely certain was the God-given Word of instruction. Here then we have an outstanding illustration of the supreme value and the practical use of the written Word of God. It provides plain indication of the governing principles of life and liberty, of true safety and well-being. It is, therefore, suicidal not to abide by the God-given Word and to obey its explicit injunctions.

Man's natural consciousness of appetite or hunger and still more the experience of actual shortage of food do not, however, make falling into sin inevitable. Rather they provide opportunity to learn the practical application of life's deeper governing principle. So God in His providence allows men to hunger in order to find out which they will put first—obedience to Him or the satisfaction of appetite. It was, indeed, from a scriptural testimony to this truth, in connection with God's dealings with the Israelites, when they, too, were in the wilderness and hungry, that our Lord quoted when He answered the devil's first temptation. For, in Dt. viii. 2, 3, it is written: '*And thou shalt remember all the way which the Lord thy God led thee these forty years in the wilderness, to humble thee, and to prove thee, to know what was in thine heart, whether thou wouldest keep his commandments, or no. And he humbled thee, and suffered thee to hunger, and fed thee with manna, which thou knewest not, neither did thy fathers know; that he might make thee know that man doth not live by bread only, but by every word that proceedeth out of the mouth of the Lord doth man live.*'

So there are times in human experience when for our safety and God's glory we must set over against the pressure of feeling and appetite the precepts and prohibitions of God's written Word. For, while man must eat to live, the first principle of life is not eating, but obedience to the laws which condition the healthy enjoyment of life. For instance, in the matter of marriage and sex relationship too much prominence often tends to be given to natural feelings and desires, and to the satisfaction of appetite or so-called 'love'—what the Bible calls the 'lust of the flesh'. What is often forgotten is the overriding sanction of the Word of God. Men too readily forget that successful marriage and healthy and happy family life can be realized only through the proper observance of those strict and sacred laws governing sex relations, which have been so plainly laid down by the Creator who instituted marriage. It is from the God-given Word, and not only from our own human and sometimes sinful and selfish instincts and emotions, that we need to learn how to preserve and to possess the true purity and potential beauty of married life.

One may, in illustration, compare a long distance express train, which has but recently started out on its journey, and is stopped by a signal at 'danger'. While the passengers may all be eager to speed on their way, while the engine may be almost bursting with steam, it would be wrong for the engine driver not to stop and to wait until the 'all-clear' sign is given. Safety in train driving is secured not by desire to arrive, nor by self-assertive unwillingness to stop or to wait, but by submission to direction. The visible witness, which reveals the condition of the unseen line ahead, deserves prompt and unquestioning obedience. Similarly the God-given Word should govern and restrain all satisfaction of human appetite and all expression of human activity.

(*b*) *Mt. iv. 5–7*

Appetite for food is not, however, the only legitimate human desire which the devil tries to degrade. There are also the spirit of adventure and the urge of ambition. For it is in the blood of some men to make ventures, to be daring; and it is a natural and healthy thing to desire to succeed and to win place or power among men. It is these stirrings of desire which give the enemy of souls corresponding opportunity to misdirect their expression. So the characteristic elements of the world of sinful humanity include not only '*the lust of the flesh*', but also '*the lust of the eyes, and the pride of life*'. These are the things which all come to nought and pass away; for they end in sin and death. In direct opposition to them it is only the man, who by abiding in the Word of God does the will of God, who himself abides for ever. (See 1 Jn. ii. 15–17.)

The remaining two temptations of our Lord show how He encountered and answered enticements to misdirect first, the spirit of adventure, and second, the urge of ambition. Let us first consider the former, the temptation to throw Himself down from a pinnacle of the temple. This was a temptation to win applause and acclamation by sensational display. It was an enticement to reckless, unjustified and potentially disastrous venture. Yet it was very subtly and attractively presented. For our Lord had just taken His stand on God's Word and confessed His faith in God's preservation. He had refused to be misled by fearful and unbelieving rationalism. So, by a master in the art of temptation, He was promptly incited to engage in an act of reckless and irrational credulity. The devil quoted a word from the Scriptures which promised divine protection. He encouraged Jesus to step out in daring venture in His chosen pathway of absolute faith in God and His Word, when actually, thus deliberately to throw Himself down would have been an act of folly and presumption, a departure from the appointed way of God for His servant in which alone He had promised to protect Him. (Note that in quoting Ps. xci. 11, 12 the devil omitted '*in all thy ways*'; for this was an enticement deliberately to depart from the way, and still to expect preservation.)

Again our Lord answered by an appeal to first principles, by quoting a plain prohibition of the written Word of God: '*Thou shalt not tempt the Lord thy God.*' Also He deliberately set the restriction imposed by this precept over against the encouragement to venture apparently afforded by the scriptural promise. He answered, '*It is written again*' or 'It is also written.' And this other Scripture made it plain that so to act would involve failure to maintain a due sense of responsibility for the stewardship of life. It would in fact have been to play the fool and to tempt Providence. One cannot violate a principle and then expect to claim a promise. So the kind of action which the devil suggested was completely ruled out.

Here there is most important truth for all to learn who are eager to live the life of Christian faith and devotion. For this temptation makes all too plain that, if the devil cannot prevent a man from being spiritual and believing, God-conscious and counting on God's promises, he will tempt him extravagantly to overdo such devotion and to lose his head and misapply some fancied scriptural guidance in some wild venture of so-called faith. It is fatally wrong to suppose that we can force God's hand to work for us by recklessly throwing ourselves down into danger. Rather it becomes God's faithful servants to keep God's way, and to wait His time to lift them up to possess the promised inheritance. (See Ps. xxxvii. 5–7, 34; Jn. xii. 32.)

(*c*) *Mt. iv. 8–11*

The devil's third temptation of our Lord was an appeal to ambition, it was based on His desire to achieve conquest. The devil was not wrong in supposing that our Lord was out for big things in the world. What he did was to suggest a quick road to success, to tempt Jesus to forsake principle for power, to sell His soul in order to gain the world, only to find if He did that He was serving not the glory of God but the lordship of the devil. Also, this experience of our Lord illustrates as no other can that such temptation may come to one whose motives are unselfish, who is out to do good.

Here our Lord at once sensed the fundamental disloyalty of treason. Such a proposal could come only from the arch-enemy of God, the supreme traitor, with whom there can be no possible compromise or parley. So Jesus engaged with him in no argument or discussion. He spoke the abrupt decisive word of dismissal, and appealed to the one supreme principle of all service, which made any response to such a proposal absolutely unthinkable. '*Then saith Jesus unto him, Get thee hence, Satan: for it is written, Thou shalt worship the Lord thy God, and him only shalt thou serve.*'

This, then, is life's primary and exclusive loyalty—to worship the Lord our God, to serve Him only. The one purpose of heeding and observing His Word is to preserve this loyalty unimpaired and to give it worthy expression. So let us notice that in each one of our Lord's three answers to temptation this conscious Godward relation is fundamental. It is this direct reference to God, to His will, His ways, and His claims, that rightly settles what a man may or may not do. Such reference is actually made in explicit relation to life's varying circumstances and frequent temptations, by the recollection, understanding and application of particular Scriptures and the underlying principles therein illustrated or enunciated. To avoid being misled by excess of zeal or credulity it is important to preserve the balance of truth by weighing Scripture against Scripture. Finally, just as the fear of God is the beginning of right understanding, so His service is the end of all true obedience. His Word deserves and demands active compliance. We ought gladly and wholeheartedly to submit to its restraints and to act under its constraints. Only so can we please God and enjoy His blessing. Only so can we '*in all these things*' of present untoward circumstance be made '*more than conquerors through him that loved us*' (Rom. viii. 37).

CHAPTER IV

OBEYING THE GOSPEL

I. THE PRINCIPLE OF THE OBEDIENCE OF FAITH

IN the world into which Adam and Eve were put, all things were of God, created by Him to fulfil His will and purpose. Adam and Eve could themselves make nothing new; nor could they alter the character of human life, and make it different by their own independent activity. They were dependent creatures. Their privilege and calling were to find their place and fulfilment in the order of God's creation, by learning His way from His Word, gladly accepting it, and diligently observing it. Disaster occurred because they departed from this obedience of faith in God and in the way of His appointment. They ceased to act on the God-given Word. In other words, the fall of man into sin was due to the disobedience of unbelief.

The fall of man brought him under God's condemnation and made him subject to death as the penalty of sin. His position was now hopeless and helpless, apart from the utterly undeserved intervention of God in redeeming grace. Man was, in fact, wholly in God's hands as the sovereign Creator and Judge; man was wholly dependent on His will and His working for all hope of salvation and life. For any redemption from sin and re-establishment in life must of necessity doubly be all of God, entirely His doing. Only if God were so pleased to act, and only if God Himself provided the remedy, was there any hope of deliverance.

So man, fallen in sin, was thrown back upon the principle he had forsaken, the principle of the obedience of faith in

God, as alone affording any hope of salvation. Consequently the gospel to be preached to sinners makes the principle of the obedience of faith doubly necessary. Not only is it the principle of enjoying life in fellowship with God, once the sinner regains it; but also it is the only principle whose operation can bring hope and help to man fallen and doomed in sin. For, if he is to be saved, God must do it, and man must wholly trust God to rescue him. Also, if he is to be saved, God must indicate the way, and provide the means, and man must submit to the directions, and accept the provision thus given, and become wholly and unquestioningly obedient. Hope dawns, therefore, for the sinner in relation to God and the gospel of saving grace, when he recommences the practice of the obedience of faith. To this he must deliberately return.

Not only, therefore, can there be no enjoyment of the blessings of the gospel without faith; but also, there can be no such enjoyment without repentance, whereby the sinner renounces the disobedience of his unbelief, and returns to the obedience of faith in God. So our Lord began His public preaching by exhorting men: '*Repent ye, and believe the gospel*' (Mk. i. 15). So Paul testified '*both to the Jews, and also to the Greeks, repentance toward God, and faith toward our Lord Jesus Christ*' (Acts xx. 21). And he declared that his gospel and '*the preaching of Jesus Christ*' was '*according to the revelation of the mystery,*' which is now '*according to the commandment of the everlasting God, made known to all nations for the obedience of faith*' (Rom. xvi. 25, 26).

Of this evangelical and saving truth concerning the purpose of God to save, and concerning man's way to enjoy the benefit of salvation, the Scriptures afford many illustrations. They all make plain that man must believe and respond to the God-given Word in the obedience of faith. For '*without faith it is impossible to please him*' (Heb. xi. 6); and '*faith without works is dead*' (Jas. ii. 26).

(*a*) *Heb. xi. 7*

In the days before the flood Noah's reverence for God and his faith in Him made him heed the warning provided by the God-given Word concerning the certain impending judgment of the flood. It also made him act on the guidance provided by the God-given Word concerning the way to be preserved from drowning. So Noah gave himself to the task of preparing an ark. By this active outgoing of faith in responsive obedience Noah not only himself found acceptance with God; he was also used to the salvation of his family. In addition, as '*a preacher of righteousness*' (2 Pet. ii. 5), he was used to give for God a witness to his generation, which served to increase the justice of the condemnation to destruction of the unbelieving and disobedient world.

(*b*) *Ex. xi. 4–7, xii. 3–13*

When the Israelites were still in bondage in Egypt, and God was purposing to bring them out to be His people, God gave to them through His servant Moses both plain warning of the impending judgment upon the firstborn of every Egyptian family, and equally plain witness of the way in which His people might find protection against corresponding judgment in their own homes. On the appointed night all the firstborn in the land of Egypt would die; but such destruction would not befall any Israelite house whose door posts had been duly sprinkled with the shed blood of a slain lamb. So said the God-given Word; and the Israelites not only believed it, they acted on it. They believed that God would do what He said; that the judgment would happen; and that the divinely appointed way of protection from it would avail, if they made use of it. So in each Israelite home the shed blood was sprinkled; and the firstborn son was saved. And all as an expression and a consequence of the faithfulness of God and of the corresponding obedience of men's faith in God.

(*c*) *Nu. xxi. 4–9*

Here we read that the Israelites in the wilderness were beset, as a judgment from God, by serpents whose bite caused many to die. They acknowledged their sin, and looked for deliverance from God alone. God gave guidance how the need was to be met, and in what way He would save those otherwise certain to die. A serpent of brass was to be made and set up on a pole. Those bitten had only to look at it to enjoy healing. Again, they acted in faith, and through such obedience found deliverance. '*And Moses made a serpent of brass, and put it upon a pole, and it came to pass, that if a serpent had bitten any man, when he beheld the serpent of brass, he lived.*'

Not only so, we find in Jn. iii. 14, 15 that our Lord Himself used this incident as an illustration of the purpose of His own crucifixion in relation to the need of perishing sinners. He was similarly to be 'lifted up', that the perishing might look to Him and be saved. So He said: '*And as Moses lifted up the serpent in the wilderness, even so must the Son of man be lifted up: That whosoever believeth in him should not perish, but have eternal life.*' Salvation, therefore, is found, according to the gospel of Christ, through the acknowledgment of our need and dire peril because of sin, and through the obedience of faith in looking wholly to Christ crucified as the one sufficient, divine provision to secure deliverance and to make new and eternal life ours.

(d) 2 Ki. v. 1–14

Naaman, the Syrian, was a leper. He was led to look for healing to the God of Israel and to His prophet Elisha. He had to learn the place and the necessity of the obedience of faith. '*So Naaman came with his horses and with his chariot, and stood at the door of the house of Elisha. And Elisha sent a messenger unto him, saying, Go and wash in Jordan seven times, and thy flesh shall come again to thee, and thou shalt be clean. But Naaman was wroth, and went away, and said, Behold, I thought, He will surely come out to me, and stand, and call on the name of the Lord his God, and strike his hand over the place, and recover the leper. Are not Abana and Pharpar, rivers of Damascus, better than all the waters of Israel? may I not wash in them, and be clean? So he turned and went away in a rage.*'

Naturally he was not attracted by the divinely appointed means and method of healing. But only when he mentally accepted it and actively submitted to it, did he find the coveted cleansing. '*Then went he down, and dipped himself seven times in Jordan, according to the saying of the man of God; and his flesh came again like unto the flesh of a little child, and he was clean.*'

Similarly we find, in the fulness of God's time, when God sent forth His Son to redeem, that many took offence at the message which was preached, because it offered salvation from sin through Christ crucified for sinners. Such a message seemed to the cultured Gentile mind ridiculous, and to the religious Jewish mind blasphemous. How could public execution as a criminal and open exposure to the curse of heaven provide salvation for the world? Yet, this is the divinely appointed way of salvation, and the divinely provided remedy for sin. '*For he hath made him to be sin for us . . . ; that we might be made the righteousness of God in him*' (2 Cor. v. 21). And this message, '*the preaching of the cross*' is the means God is pleased to use '*to save them that believe*'. (See 1 Cor. i. 18–25.)

The only sufficient and indispensable condition for enjoying the benefit of the gospel of saving grace is, therefore, the obedience of faith, that is, believing God means what He says and acting accordingly with hope fixed only and wholly upon Him and upon His faithful doing.

II. THE DEAD HEAR HIS VOICE

The word offered to sinful men in the gospel is fundamentally a word of cleansing and quickening, offering forgiveness and new life. This is a word which is humanly impossible of fulfilment. Such a word can effectively be spoken only by God, who can both forgive sin and bring something out of nothing in new creation. For He can quicken the dead; and so He calls the things which are not as though they are. This is the God who spoke to the fatherless Abram, the man with a childless wife, who was already past the normal age for bearing children, and re-named him '*Abraham*', saying, '*I have made thee a father of many nations.*' And Abram believed God, and was henceforth called '*Abraham*'. Like the justified, who are reckoned righteous because of their faith in God, so Abraham was reckoned to be what as yet he was not. Also, by the obedience of faith he possessed the actual fulfilment of God's Word. He became a father; indeed, in thus believing God, he became the father of all who believe from every nation. (See Rom. iv. 16–22.)

So the divine word of the gospel, which sinners are to believe and to obey in order to be saved, is not only a word which directs and commands—as when Naaman was sent to the River Jordan to wash and be clean. Its very utterance also implies and guarantees accompanying divine provision and enablement to make its fulfilment possible. Those who respond to it are in the first place not those who do anything to merit salvation, but rather those to whom something transforming or regenerating is done; for only if this is so can they fulfil the activity of faith's obedience. Once again let us turn to the Scripture for some illustrations.

(*a*) *Mt. xii. 10a, 13*

'*And, behold, there was a man which had his hand withered.*' Here there is introduced to us a man who had clearly lost all power of using one of his hands. The one thing he could not do was to move it, and to bring it into full action like the other hand. Yet this very thing which he could not do was the thing which the Saviour and the great Physician told him to do. '*Then saith he to the man, Stretch forth thine hand.*' And in the obedience of faith the man did the humanly and naturally impossible. '*And he stretched it forth; and it was restored whole, like as the other.*' Similarly, when those powerless to serve God's will hear the Word of God in the gospel, in the obedience of faith they begin to do that which, without the re-creative power of God, would be utterly impossible. The outworked enjoyment of the inwrought benefit becomes theirs in the activity of faith's obedience. Henceforth their testimony is, '*He spake, and it was done.*' (See Ps. xxxiii. 9.)

(*b*) *Mk. ii. 1–12*

In the incident of the healing of the helpless paralytic, who was carried to Jesus by four other men, and let down through the roof of a house to the feet of Jesus, an event of the same kind happened again. The man was told by Jesus to do the one thing he could not do—to arise, and take up his bed, and walk home. His immediate performance of this humanly impossible action was explicitly made by our Lord into a sign and proof of the man's release from the guilt and power of sin, and, more particularly, of our Lord's own authority to grant such release. Because of His power as the

Son of man over realms completely outside ordinary man's control, He was, and is, able to speak the kind of enabling Word, which opens up before the man who responds to it a new experience of both cleansing and quickening, of remission, and regeneration. So, as in the case of the helpless and sin-stained paralytic, response to this Word and its Author in the obedience of faith both brings the sinner into the enjoyment of peace with God, and brings the impotent into the experience of power to walk in God's way.

(*c*) *Mk. v. 35–43; Lk. vii. 11–17; Jn. xi. 38–46*

Outstanding illustrations of this truth that in the preaching of the gospel the dead hear God's voice were provided by our Lord on the three occasions when He restored to life the physically dead. On each occasion He addressed the dead body, and commanded the dead person to arise or come forth; and on each occasion he or she acted accordingly. Living reappearance and return to ordinary human living immediately followed. Here clearly our Lord spoke as one able to reach and to quicken into responsive action those who otherwise were beyond the reach of human calling, and were themselves unable to come back into life in the body. So, the word to which these dead responded was a word which carried with it the prevailing authority and the quickening power adequate for its actual fulfilment. Those who heard it obviously believed it and the Lord who said it, and they visibly obeyed both it and Him.

Such illustrations help to confirm our understanding of the truth that the obedience of faith, which God commands in the gospel, is not only an obedience which He desires should be rendered, but also an obedience which God therewith makes possible. Consequently the obedience of saving faith is more than the way of man's response in order to enjoy the blessings of the gospel; it is rather the new way of man's response to God, which is made possible by the gospel, or rather by God in the gospel. For He provides the grace or new life for its performance. Those, therefore, who obey this word of saving grace come to know that such activity of faith is no work or merit of theirs, but something possible only and wholly by the gift of God. In other words, this means that to set ourselves to live the life of faith's obedience to God's Word is but to seek to work out that salvation, which is first wrought for us and within us by God Himself. (See Phil. ii. 12, 13.)

The Word of God which comes to sinful men in the gospel is, therefore, like the voice of someone saying to a blind man in the dark, 'Read this', and simultaneously making reading possible by giving him both sight and light. It is like someone throwing wide a prison door as he says to the man confined within, 'Come out.' It is, as we have seen, like someone confronting a corpse, and saying to the departed dead person, 'Arise'; and he gets up. Indeed, only a word from God which is thus accompanied by His gift of light and freedom and life can offer an effective way of present salvation to men who are blind and bound and dead in sin. It is to such a word and to such a God that sinners are invited, or rather commanded, in the gospel to render the obedience of faith.

'*Verily, verily, I say unto you,*' said Jesus, '*He that heareth my word, and believeth on him that sent me, hath everlasting life, and shall not come into condemnation; but is passed from death unto life. Verily, verily, I say unto you, The hour is coming, and now is, when the dead shall hear the voice of the Son of God: and they that hear shall live.*' (Jn. v. 24, 25.) '*Wherefore he saith, Awake thou that sleepest, and arise from the dead, and Christ shall give thee light.*' (Eph. v. 14.)

CHAPTER V

TRUE DISCIPLESHIP

I. THE SIGNIFICANCE OF JOHN VIII. 31, 32

THE principle of the obedience of faith in God and in His Word is not only the principle of entering into life; it is also the principle of enjoying life and finding its true fulfilment. In other words, it is the principle not only of obtaining salvation from sin, but also of all subsequent true discipleship of Christ as Lord.

When our Lord called men to follow Him and to become His disciples, the characteristic which He expected most was implicit response to His word in faith and obedience. So He broke into men's lives with the one absolute demand, *Follow me;* and He was satisfied, and indeed worthily answered, only when men left all and followed Him. To such followers He made it unmistakably plain that He expected unquestioning acceptance of His teaching and wholehearted action in obedience to it. He declared to such men that they would show their real attitude to His Person by such obedience to His Word. He explicitly commanded that all who were subsequently made disciples should be taught to observe all things which He had commanded. (See Mt. xxviii. 19, 20.)

Let us consider His own statement of the condition of true discipleship: '*Jesus therefore said to those Jews which had believed him, If ye abide in my word, then are ye truly my disciples; and ye shall know the truth, and the truth shall make you free*' (Jn. viii. 31, 32, R.V.).

It is instructive to notice when and to whom our Lord

thus stated this condition of discipleship. It was to Jews who had reached the point of believing Him. The significance of this is that it indicates that, for those who would acknowledge Christ with a willingness to learn from Him, there is a point at the very beginning at which He demands that unquestioning loyalty should take the place of criticism. Critical inquiry and honest investigation are right and commendable as a means to discover the truth about Jesus. But once I know who He is, once I have reached the place where evidence demands that I recognize Him as trustworthy, then He asks nothing less than uncompromising and unconditional loyalty.

Indeed, no other method is possible. He cannot accept disciples who want themselves to choose the course and method of instruction. In His school these things are already fixed and cannot be altered to suit the fancy or preferences of men. He cannot accept followers who want themselves to choose the path and set the lead. That was the nature of the issue when He spoke as He did to the Jews. Many Jews expected the Messiah, but they had their own ideas of what He ought to do. What some really hoped to do was to make the Messiah their servant, and to use His supernatural power to achieve their own ends. But such ideas the Christ Himself could not fulfil. (See, for example, Jn. vi. 15.) He had His own unalterable God-given plans. Those who would follow Him must accept His word as their law, otherwise unity of action would be impossible.

This issue is still a vital one for all who would be true disciples of Christ. For His ways are not our ways; and we cannot be true disciples unless we learn to give up our own ideas and to accept His. Consequently, as soon as men recognized who He was, and confessed their belief in Him, He confronted them with this necessary condition of progress in discipleship—*Abide in my word.* He cannot ask the world at large thus to accept His word and to act on it, because such men do not believe in Him; but He does make this demand of those who know who He is.

What if we do thus abide in His word? He promises that we shall know the truth, and that the truth will make us free. It is as we hold to, and act on, the truth which we do know that we discover or discern more of the truth. We are thus delivered from our own prejudices and misconceptions which would otherwise mislead us or hold us in bondage. Also we secure for ourselves the guarantee of continuance in our doing. For the Word of God abides for ever. (See 1 Pet. i. 23.) And if we make room for it to abide in us, if we ourselves, no matter how much we are pushed or enticed to depart from it, if we ourselves abide in it, we shall remain and so will our deeds, when others perish. For the man who abides in the Word of God and thus becomes the man who does the will of God is the man who abides for ever. (See 1 Jn. ii. 17.)

II. THE EXAMPLE OF SIMON PETER

The faithful record in the Gospel story of Peter's denial of his Lord is surely meant to make us pointedly aware that personal discipleship of Christ may begin right, persist long, achieve much, and yet go fundamentally wrong, and need radical re-orientation and renewal. Let us see then what we can learn from this story concerning the condition of true discipleship.

(*a*) *Lk. v. 1–11*

As a disciple, Simon Peter began rightly. Luke's record here shows us this in out-worked practice. Here in the world of fishing, where he might have claimed to know all there was to know, and where a whole night's failure to catch fish suggested to natural judgment that it was foolish to try now, Simon immediately accepted the imperative word of Jesus as sufficient and decisive. '*Master*,' he answered—and let us note the word—'*Master, we have toiled all the night, and have taken nothing: nevertheless at thy word I will let down the net.*' Nor was he thereby misled and disappointed. For '*when they had this done, they inclosed a great multitude of fishes*'. So Simon Peter exhibited in action his obedient faith in the Master's word, and its satisfying reward.

(*b*) *Mt. xvi. 15, 16, 21–23*

Yet this exemplary disciple, so ready, when challenged, to confess his personal acknowledgement of Jesus as the Christ of God, went surprisingly wrong when the Master began the second stage of His instruction. For, once His Person was fully confessed by His chosen band of disciples, the Master went on to a second subject in His teaching. '*From that time forth began Jesus to shew unto his disciples, how that he must go unto Jerusalem, and suffer many things of the elders and chief priests and scribes, and be killed, and be raised again the third day.*' Peter met this announcement not with the submissive acceptance of a true disciple but with the assertive and presumptuous rejection of a self-confident critic. '*Then Peter took him, and began to rebuke him, saying, Be it far from thee, Lord: this shall not be unto thee.*'

Such a complete change of attitude towards the Master happened when and where one would least expect it. It appeared in the leading disciple, shortly after he had made a personal and divinely inspired confession of Christ's Person. Also, its sinful and satanic character was the less suspected, because in intention it was so well-meaning. For Peter's protest was, as he saw it, made on the highest religious grounds. Was it not his religious duty to protest? Did not the

Scriptures foretell glory and sovereignty for God's Christ? Surely it was a shameful contradiction of His proper destiny for Him to be put to death!

So Peter became involved, without realizing it (as not a few have done in our own day), in a fatal contradiction of attitude. He still called Jesus 'Lord'; and yet he openly opposed His Word and rejected His way. Nor did the Master hide from Peter the gravity of such a change of attitude. He immediately and bluntly rebuked Peter for becoming an agent and mouthpiece of the devil, and a stumbling-block in the way of the Master's progress; and all because he preferred his own human ideas to explicit divine statement.

(*c*) *Mt. xxvi. 69–75*

Peter did not heed the warning. He failed to comprehend not only its gravity, but even its truth. He went on blindly with a divided mind. He still was sure that Jesus was the Christ. But he would not have a Christ who must go to the cross. It was surely this divided mind that ultimately involved him in disowning his discipleship of Jesus as the Christ. For the unwanted suffering, so explicitly and repeatedly predicted, inevitably drew near. Jesus was arrested, mocked, ill-treated. Peter was asked whether he were not one of those who had followed Jesus as the Christ. '*A damsel came unto him, saying, Thou also wast with Jesus of Galilee. But he denied before them all, saying, I know not what thou sayest.*' And all because he had earlier and repeatedly refused to take to heart the God-given Word which was intended to prepare his mind to accept what he naturally did not want, but what God had eternally fore-ordained.

(*d*) *Jn. xiii. 3–9*

The Master, however, knew that deep down underneath Peter's heart intention was right. He coveted glory and honour, not suffering and shame, for God's Christ. He had to learn that the shame was necessary first, and necessary as the price of his own salvation. So the loving Lord, who saw the inevitable denial that was impending, did not disown him as a disciple, and treat him as an unbeliever. Rather He prayed for him that his faith should not fail. (See Lk. xxii. 31, 32.) Also, He brought the fundamental issue home to Peter in the object lesson of the feet-washing. For when Jesus took a towel and a basin and began to wash His disciples' feet, Peter once more objected, and fundamentally for the same reason that he objected to the coming cross, because he wanted to save his Master from humiliation. But, said Jesus in effect, the thing which you do not want, and cannot now understand, is the thing which is necessary for your benefit. Without it you cannot share in the kingdom of God. '*If I wash thee not, thou hast no part with me.*' Faced with this ultimatum Peter returned to the proper attitude of discipleship, and accepted what as yet he did not understand, because the Lord said that it must be.

Nor is this story without its continuing application to many present-day disciples. There are still those who begin rightly in the simplicity of the unquestioning obedience of faith. But later, in the realm of the intellectual understanding of God's Word and God's ways, and the recognition of the necessity of Christ's substitutionary and penal death for the salvation of sinners, they are beset by difficulties, and even make their outspoken objections. Often, when their mind is thus wrongly divided, their heart is at bottom, like Peter's, still right. For such, return to harmony of mind and heart through understanding of God's way, and enjoyment of its saving benefit, can come, as it came to Peter, only through fresh submission to the God-given Word. This is for them, as for us all, the abiding condition of true discipleship.

CHAPTER VI

PERILS IN THE WAY

IT is plain from the Old Testament and the New Testament alike that what God desires in His people is that they should be doers of the word and not hearers only. (See Jas. i. 22, 25.) It was in such terms that Moses charged Israel before his own death, and before they entered the promised land. So we read: '*Now therefore hearken, O Israel, unto the statutes and unto the judgments, which I teach you, for to do them, that ye may live, and go in and possess the land which the Lord God of your fathers giveth you*' (Dt. iv. 1; cf. v. 1, vi. 1, viii. 1, xi. 1, 32, xii. 1).

In thus exhorting them to do the truth of God, Moses also exhorted them to take particular care to do the whole truth, and to do nothing but the truth. In other words, he warned them both against including what God had not ordained, and against omitting what God had commanded. For only so could they properly and fully keep His commandments. So we read: '*Ye shall not add unto the word which I command you, neither shall ye diminish ought from it, that ye may keep the commandments of the Lord your God which I command you*'; and again later we read, '*What thing soever I command you, observe to do it: thou shalt not add thereto, nor diminish from it*' (Dt. iv. 2, xii. 32). Similarly the closing words of Revelation, with which in God's providential ordering the New Testament ends, threaten the solemn eternal judgment of God upon any man who shall add to, or take away from, the words of this book. (See Rev. xxii. 18, 19.) These, therefore, are persistent perils. Let us consider them each in turn.

I. ADDING TO THE WORD OF GOD

The danger of adding to the Word of God is a danger which besets people who are active in works of religious devotion. It is a subtle peril which besets the religiously minded, and often overtakes them unawares. It is the danger of the ritualistic and the superstitious. It is the danger of the legalistic and conscientious, who put themselves under obligation to perform certain practices or to keep certain rules which are not of divine appointment, and whose performance does not please God or truly profit men. Let us seek to take to heart the admonition of some scriptural examples.

(*a*) *Is. xxix. 13*

This tendency to add something not of divine appointment but of human devising may find expression in the professed worship of God Himself. So Isaiah was given a word from God to utter about the worship of the people of his day. '*The Lord said . . . their fear towards me is taught by the precept of men.*' In other words, the forms they used to express professed reverence for God were man-made not God-ordained; and their virtual condemnation here by the prophet implies that they involved practices displeasing to God.

(*b*) *Dt. iv. 9–12, 15, 16, 23, 24*

Moses indeed gave a specific warning against this very peril in the charge whose opening words we have already quoted. He reminded them that the special revelation from God, which was granted to them at Sinai, was meant to teach them how to worship Him, and how to bring up their children to do the same. What they needed to remember was that in this revelation of God they '*heard the voice of the words, but saw no similitude*'. God made Himself known not in visible form but in intelligible utterance. Therefore in the congregation of His people, gathered to worship Him, they should beware of the natural desire to have some visible object or image towards which reverence can be physically directed. It is rather by prophetic utterance, by the preaching of the Word, that God is pleased to make men aware of His presence in their midst, and to call forth the worship of their adoration and believing response. So Paul wrote concerning the meeting of a Christian congregation: '*But if all prophesy, and there come in one that believeth not, or one unlearned, he is convinced of all, he is judged of all; And thus are the secrets of his heart made manifest; and so falling down on his face, he will worship God, and report that God is in you of a truth*' (1 Cor. xiv. 24, 25). We need to beware, therefore, lest in our Christian congregations, out of a natural desire to help worship, we wrongly add what God has not ordained. For the 'idol' that is given the worship that rightly belongs to God alone is an abomination in His sight. Such worship, Moses said, '*the Lord thy God hath forbidden thee.*' Nor let Israel forget that '*the Lord thy God is a consuming fire, even a jealous God*'.

(*c*) *Mt. xv. 1–9*

Our Lord condemned some of the religious practices of His day for the same reason, and in the strongest terms. When asked by the scribes and Pharisees why His disciples broke certain recognized religious observances, He charged them with introducing man-made precepts to the exclusion of the proper observance of God-given commandments. '*Thus have ye,*' He said, '*made the commandment of God of none effect by your tradition.*' So He called them '*hypocrites*' or play-actors, acting a part which was not an expression of their real selves; and He endorsed the words of Isaiah as applying to them that '*This people draweth nigh unto me with their mouth, and honoureth me with their lips; but their heart is far from me. But in vain they do worship me, teaching for doctrines the commandments of men.*'

Thus our Lord Himself taught that in the practice of religion man-made additions can completely invalidate the revealed truth of God and make His Word virtually inoperative. Nor did this grievous corruption occur in the midst of heathen darkness but in the place of special religious privilege, in the place of revelation and God-given enlightenment, and among those professedly learned in the law of God and responsible to teach others of His ways. Nor has so-called Christendom been free from similar corruption, of which the Roman Church is an outstanding example. For they have plainly added many things to the written Word of God, and have often made its plain sense and the wonderful gospel of divine grace of none effect by their tradition.

II. TAKING AWAY FROM THE WORD OF GOD

The opposite danger is the danger of diminishing or taking away, the danger of failing to accept and to respond to the whole Word of God. This in our Lord's day was a peril which had overtaken the Sadducees, who said that there was '*no resurrection, neither angel, nor spirit*' (Acts xxiii. 8). This is a danger which besets people who are intellectually active and are influenced by some prevailing philosophy or some school of thought of their day. It is the danger of the rationalist, the liberal, the modernist, who is unwilling to be bound by '*the faith which was once for all delivered unto the saints*' (Jude 3, R.V.). It is the danger of the student, who in the name of honest scientific investigation and inquiry for truth is persuaded to indulge in what is often presumptuous and vain theorizing. Again, let us seek to heed the warning of specific scriptural examples.

(*a*) *1 Tim. vi. 20, 21*

Here Timothy is told plainly and urgently that if he is to preserve faithfully the deposit of revealed truth, the very Word of God with which he has been entrusted, he must deliberately turn away from the godless or blasphemous nonsense and the speculative propositions and counter-arguments of those who in the name of so-called 'science' are opposing and abandoning the revealed truth of God. Timothy needs, it is implied, to beware of being fascinated and captivated by their pretensions to originality or thoroughness. His very love of the truth of God should give him an instinctive distaste for, and an aversion from, the error which opposes it.

For in such a situation the only alternative to allowing one's devotion to God-given truth to govern one's reaction is for oneself to be captured by some opposing new school of thought. While some still profess their continued loyalty to the God-given Word, others may profess their loyalty to some prevailing scientific theory. For example, they may become 'evolutionists' or 'dialectical materialists'. The result is that such a theory, once thus professed, influences and reorientates their whole outlook. Such people no longer see things as they used to do. They cease to be simple believers in the God-given Word. They no longer hold to, or are held by, plain scriptural doctrines. As far as the true faith of Christ is concerned, they err and go astray.

(*b*) *2 Tim. ii. 16–18*

Here the same warning is repeated, with more particular reference to specific error, to individuals who propagate it, and to the harm it must do. Such empty and godless theorizing only promotes a decrease of true reverence for God. It tends to create a wrong atmosphere for study and worthy appreciation; sacred things cease to be sacred. Not only so, the particular theory thus fancied becomes dominant; and so men pay reverence, not to God and His Word, but to human authorities and '*their word*'. In contrast to God's Word which brings life and health or can be eaten as nourishing food, this 'word' is like a malignant gangrene, which eats its way into healthy organisms, and works death and destruction. An illustration of such influence is found in Hymenaeus and Philetus and their teaching. For on the strength of their scientific theorizing or philosophical presuppositions they had apparently denied the possibility of a future resurrection of the body, and had thus robbed some of a precious fundamental of true Christian faith. Such taking away from the God-given Word is dishonouring to God and harmful to men.

(*c*) *Acts xx. 30, 32*

Finally, we need to notice again that such dangers can arise within the Church. It is from among the company of professed and baptized believers that some may thus themselves go wrong, and then lead others astray. So Paul warned the elders of the Church in Ephesus: '*Also of your own selves shall men arise, speaking perverse things, to draw away disciples after them.*' Here there is warning of the same snare as we have noticed above. Such false teachers entice men and women to become, not true disciples of Christ, but followers of themselves, and propagators of their false teaching.

For their safety and true edification Paul commended the Ephesian elders '*to God, and to the word of his grace*'. It is through unquestioning faith in this God and this Word, and through persistent obedience to Him and to it, without addition or diminution, that we, too, may find our way both to protection from error and to progress in the truth.

CHAPTER VII

THE PRACTICE OF OBEDIENCE (1)

THOSE who would set themselves to make the response of faith's obedience to God and His Word soon find that they are involved in an activity which makes exacting and unceasing demands, which embrace the whole of living, and continue until the end of life's journey. Indeed, in the Christian experience nothing falls outside its concern. It is, therefore, impossible here to engage on any exhaustive treatment of the subject of this chapter. All we shall attempt (in the next chapter as well as in this one) is to consider some of the demands which such obedience makes on those who would sustain its performance.

1. ENDURANCE

This activity of obedience is an indispensable expression of a living faith. Without it faith is a worthless profession. What is more, the full response of faith to the God-given Word involves not only immediate obedience but also its persistent continuance to the end. We are called not only to begin but also to complete the course, to '*run with patience*,' or endurance, '*the race that is set before us*' (Heb. xii. 1). Such continuing response to God's Word may be of two kinds. Sometimes God's Word demands active obedience to its command or constraint. At other times it requires passive submission to its plain statement of truth, prohibition or restraint. But in both kinds of response alike full possession of the reward of obedience commonly involves holding on, whether in action or submission, till God's time for fulfilment comes. Such experience puts to the proof the faith which inspires our obedience. Thus the testing of our faith demands, and is meant to produce, patience or continuance in well-doing; and only if such patience, or endurance, is allowed to bring its work to completion, can we ourselves reach the intended goal, or possess the promised inheritance.

So we read: '*My brethren, count it all joy when ye fall into divers temptations* (or 'manifold trials', R.V.)*; Knowing this, that the trying of your faith worketh patience. But let patience have her perfect work, that ye may be perfect and entire, wanting* (or 'lacking in', R.V.) *nothing*' (Jas. i. 2–4). And again: '*And we desire that every one of you do shew the same diligence to the full assurance of hope unto the end: That ye be not slothful, but followers of them who through faith and patience inherit the promises*' (Heb. vi. 11, 12).

The danger is lest, in the midst of the pathway of faith's obedience, we give up its pursuit and fail to reach the intended goal. To Christians thus tempted to turn aside in the middle, and to abandon the continuance of faith's active expression in obedience, the writer of the Epistle to the Hebrews wrote: '*Cast not away therefore your confidence, which hath great recompence of reward. For ye have need of patience, that, after ye have done the will of God, ye might receive the promise*' (Heb. x. 35, 36). Let us then consider in detail some scriptural illustrations from which we may learn these two things; first, the need for the obedience which faith inspires to be sustained to the end; and second, the inevitability of such faith being tested in order that its capacity for successful endurance may stand revealed.

(*a*) *Heb. xi. 30*

'*By faith the walls of Jericho fell down, after they were compassed about seven days.*' This brief statement refers to the familiar story of the capture of Jericho by the Israelites, a story recorded at length in Jos. vi. The significant fact was that the victory was God-given. He made the walls of Jericho to fall down flat. This conquest was possessed by the Israelites through the obedience of faith. But, unlike those bitten by snakes in the wilderness, who were immediately healed when they looked at the brazen serpent, they did not experience the victory at once. On this occasion faith had to sustain the activity of obedience to the divine command for a full seven days. Only after this persistence of believing obedience was complete did the walls fall down. Thus it is plain that progress in possession of the promised land depended upon the endurance of faith's obedience. This illustrates the governing principle of all true progress in Christian discipleship. One needs not only a faith which obeys God's Word, but also a faith which keeps on obeying. One needs not only a faith which looks to God in hope, but also a faith which is content to wait in confident expectation until God's time for fulfilment comes. So God's prophet was inspired to utter words such as, '*He that believeth shall not make haste*'; and '*Blessed are all they that wait for him*' (Is. xxviii. 16, xxx. 18).

(*b*) *Mt. viii. 23–27*

See also Mk. iv. 35-41; Lk. viii. 22–25. Trouble and danger quickly reveal the strength or weakness of one's professed confidence. Its capacity or inability to endure the strain of possible severe testing is thus discovered; and by such experience faith itself is disciplined, developed and matured. In the incident recorded here there is an illustration of faith being tested and found wanting or incomplete. The disciples followed Jesus into a ship. They went on board, not by their own initiative or decision, but as disciples following the Master. It was, therefore, by His leading that they were on the sea. Consequently the Lord Himself was responsible for the safety and the issues of the crossing.

Indeed, He Himself had assured them of the destination in view, when He said, '*Let us go over unto the other side*.' Yet, when a great storm suddenly overtook them, the disciples abandoned the faith of true discipleship in which they came on board. They lost their proper confidence. Panic stricken and afraid they awoke their sleeping Master, and virtually accused Him of indifference. 'Master, carest thou not? we perish!' The Master quickly asserted His sovereign command over wind and wave. He spoke the word, 'Be still'; and there was a great calm. The storm was no cause of alarm or fear to Him. But what did distress and disappoint Him was the failure of His disciples' faith. So, since He had them alone and away from onlookers who might overhear, He bluntly rebuked them. '*Why are ye so fearful?*' He asked. '*How is it that ye have no faith?*' How often do we not deserve similar rebuke? Not in the spirit of unbelief and fear can God's Word be obeyed, its assurance enjoyed, and its promise possessed.

(*c*) *Acts xxiii. 11, xxvii. 20–25, 44b*

A similar story, but one recording a better response of faith on the part of the Christian pilgrim, is to be found in Acts xxvii. For, while on the journey to Rome as a prisoner, Paul was involved in a prolonged storm of such severity that in the natural human judgment of those on board the ship '*all hope that we should be saved was then taken away*'. Yet Paul did not lose hope. He held on to the God-given Word, and found in it assurance of deliverance. For, long before this journey began, while Paul was still in Jerusalem, the Lord had said to him, '*Be of good cheer, Paul: for as thou hast testified of me in Jerusalem, so must thou bear witness also at Rome*.' So Paul believed that, if he was to bear witness in Rome, he could not perish on the journey thither; he must be saved out of the storm. Now, on the storm-tossed ship, not only was this hope confirmed, but also the assurance was added that all his fellow-travellers would be saved, too. So Paul stood forth openly on the deck to cheer up his dejected and despairing fellow-travellers, by giving them the outspoken testimony of faith's expectation. '*I exhort you,*' he said, '*to be of good cheer: for there shall be no loss of any man's life among you, but of the ship. For there stood by me this night the angel of God, whose I am, and whom I serve, saying, Fear not, Paul; thou must be brought before Caesar: and, lo, God hath given thee all them that sail with thee. Wherefore, sirs, be of good cheer: for I believe God, that it shall be even as it was told me.*' Nor was this a vain fancy, the delusion of wishful thinking. '*It came to pass, that they escaped all safe to land.*'

(*d*) 2 *Ki. iv.* 8–37

The story of the Shunammite woman recorded here affords an even more outstanding illustration of holding on without wavering to an assurance previously given. For, in fulfilment of the Word of the Lord, spoken to her by the prophet Elisha, this woman was given a son. After a few years the child died. What did the mother do? She did not bury the child; she went up and laid the dead body on the bed of the man of God. Why? She was throwing back responsibility to the place where it belonged. Her attitude was that, if God and His prophet had given her a child when natural hope of children was at an end, it was, so to speak, their responsibility and not hers to complete what they had begun, and to put right what had apparently gone fatally wrong in the middle. For, to such a woman, the promise of a son meant the continuation of the family through his descendants. So she held on to the faith of the beginnings of her motherhood, the faith in which the child was born.

This attitude of holding on to the assurance that this thing was a divine undertaking, and not a mere human and personal responsibility, gave her peace and hope where otherwise there would have been none. Leaving the dead body on the prophet's bed, she set off at once to find the man of God himself to commit the matter to him. To others she would betray no anxiety, for the burden was not hers but his. Why then should she be anxious? She answered, 'Peace; all is well.' But as soon as she got to Elisha himself, she threw all the burden on him, and would not leave him to go back to the child without him. For the child was not hers by her desire but by the man of God's promise. Therefore, he must come to save; and he did. The woman took back her son alive from the hands of Elisha.

Hers is an example to be followed. Often hopes seem to fail, or even to come to an end, before they have reached maturity and fulfilment. The temptation then is to let go faith, to give up hope. This is how the Israelites failed on the wilderness road between Egypt and Canaan. The success of winning through the trials of the journey between the birth of first beginnings and the full-grown manhood of completed purpose comes only to those who, like the Shunammite woman, refuse to abandon God-given assurance. '*For we are made partakers of Christ, if we hold the beginning of our confidence stedfast unto the end*' (Heb. iii. 14).

II. UNRESERVED CONFIDENCE IN GOD

No man will thus hold on in the pathway of faith's obedience, unless he has complete confidence in God's faithfulness. He must know whom He has believed, and be absolutely sure that He will keep His word. For God cannot deny Himself. As Balaam said long ago: '*God is not a man, that he should lie; neither the son of man, that he should repent: hath he said, and shall he not do it? or hath he spoken, and shall he not make it good?*' (Nu. xxiii. 19). Similarly the God-inspired Word given to comfort the believing and obedient soul that is weary and despondent, because his road is temporarily all dark, strikes the same emphasis. For in such circumstances the only satisfying activity is to rest on God and to count on His faithfulness. So we read: '*Who is among you that feareth the Lord, that obeyeth the voice of his servant, that walketh in darkness, and hath no light? let him trust in the name of the Lord, and stay upon his God*' (Is. l. 10).

(*a*) *Rom. iv. 17–21*

Abraham, the man of faith, exemplifies this spirit in an outstanding way. He was sure that God would not promise anything unless He both could do it, and also actually intended to do it. So, in utterly hopeless natural circumstances, and through prolonged delay and human disappointment, he hopefully believed. Thus Isaac was born. '*And so, after he had patiently endured, he obtained the promise*' (Heb. vi. 15).

(*b*) *Heb. xi. 17–19*

Nor is this all. For God allowed Abraham to be still further tested. The man whose hopes of the fulfilment of God's promises concerning his seed were all invested in Isaac, heard the call to offer him up as a burnt-offering. But how could he? How could he sacrifice Isaac, when it meant putting an end to all his hopes—hopes which were not of sight, but of faith, and not of men but of God? If God intended to make Isaac's posterity a great nation, how could He mean Abraham to put Isaac to death? To natural reckoning the two things were contradictory and irreconcilable. But, because he knew in whom he was believing, Abraham knew that, if he acted in obedience, and performed the deed which would put an end to all his hopes, then, because he had obeyed God, God must do something to make the impossible possible.

Consequently, under the pressure of such an apparently insoluble problem, the hope of resurrection was born. For, if the fulfilment of God's promises necessitated Isaac being alive, and yet obedience to God had demanded that Isaac must first die, then God must be going to bring him to life again. So did faith reckon; and so is undreamt-of, supernatural hope born to faith when continuance in obedience to God and His Word brings natural hope to an end.

Such obedience is therefore the way of faith's full possession. And the secret of thus going on in obedience, when obedience seems to shut us in, to darken our way, and even to threaten the loss of everything, is faith in the promises of God, and faith in God the Promiser who is sure to fulfil His Word. '*Faithful is he that calleth you, who also will do*' (1 Thes. v. 24). For when we respond to the call of His Word, not only do we move in obedience, God also moves to fulfil His Word. The hope of safe emergence from the trial, the hope of successful possession of faith's reward, rests on God's doing not on ours. As we trust and obey, and venture all on Him, God carries us through. Nor is there any other way to reach the goal of His purpose and to enjoy the best blessings of His giving. Indeed, the very pressure of God's hand in the discipline of life's circumstances constrains us, by shutting us in, to find this way of faith's obedience as the only way out.

> 'But we never can prove
> The delights of His love,
> Until all on the altar we lay;
> For the favour He shows,
> And the joy He bestows,
> Are for them who will trust and obey.'

III. A GOOD CONSCIENCE

The man who would thus prove God's faithfulness must expect to have his own faithfulness put to the proof by the God with whom he is brought into fellowship. For no man can fully enter into the satisfaction of taking God at His Word, and of enjoying the fulfilment of His promises, unless by God's grace he becomes the kind of person whose own word can be trusted and whose corresponding action can be counted on. In other words, the man who would truly obey God's Word must do so with absolute singleness and sincerity of heart; and this sincerity must be demonstrated in deed as well as in word by his diligent wholehearted observance of God's commandments. This means, to quote the psalmist's language, that he must '*walk uprightly*' (Ps. lxxxiv. 11).

(a) *Am. v. 14, 15, 21–24; Mi. vi. 6–8*

Here there is no room for compromise or hypocrisy. Outward profession and superficial practice of religious devotion, which are unsupported by serious heart intention and by corresponding upright behaviour are only hateful to God and unsatisfying to men; they deceive none but those absorbed in doing them. To this the Scriptures bear repeated witness. For instance, God spoke through Amos to the Israel of his day, and said: '*Seek good, and not evil, that ye may live: and so the Lord, the God of hosts, shall be with you, as ye have spoken. Hate the evil, and love the good, and establish judgment in the gate: it may be that the Lord God of hosts will be gracious unto the remnant of Joseph.*' And again, '*I hate, I despise your feast days, and I will not smell in your solemn assemblies. Though ye offer me burnt offerings and your meat offerings, I will not accept them: neither will I regard the peace offerings of your fat beasts. Take thou away from me the noise of thy songs; for I will not hear the melody of thy viols. But let judgment run down as waters, and righteousness as a mighty stream.'*

Or similarly Micah prophesied: '*Wherewith shall I come before the Lord, and bow myself before the high God? shall I come before him with burnt offerings, with calves of a year old? Will the Lord be pleased with thousands of rams, or with ten thousands of rivers of oil? shall I give my firstborn for my transgression, the fruit of my body for the sin of my soul? He hath shewed thee, O man, what is good; and what doth the Lord require of thee, but to do justly, and to love mercy, and to walk humbly with thy God?*'

(*b*) *1 Tim. i. 3–7*

The man who obeys God's Word must become a man whose life is wholly devoted to the expression of true love towards God and man. There can be no question that this truth is supported by the cumulative witness of both Old and New Testaments. But such love cannot be practised where heart sincerity is lacking. So Paul said, with reference to his solemn exhortation to Timothy, '*But the end of the charge is love out of a pure heart and a good conscience and faith unfeigned*' (R.V.). Such a statement explicitly indicates that there are searching moral conditions of true spiritual devotion. Deep down within one must mean what one professes without pretence or superficiality. One must be careful and active conscientiously to live up to all the light which one has. One's motive must be single and sincere, undivided and undefiled.

What is equally plain is that the possession of such purity of heart and life, or the maintenance of its unceasing pursuit, depends upon the attitude and action of the individual believer. It is possible for him to abandon the maintenance of such standards. He may, for instance, turn aside to interests and activities which still have to do with the God-given Word, but which are not in the pathway of its true obedience. He may even satisfy his desire to become a teacher in such matters, only to become engaged in activities which are inevitably profitless. Indeed, Paul plainly indicates here that such interests issue only in unprofitable arguing about supposed problems, and in the discussion of empty trivialities, instead of in promoting the divinely intended upbuilding of God's people in the way of faith. Or, as H. P. Liddon put it, such studies 'do more to suggest points for controversy than to illustrate the divine dispensation (of redemption), which is only understood in the sphere of faith'. What this kind of person needs to learn is that there is a right and a wrong use to be made of the law of God, and that it proves its excellence and brings benefit to the user only when it is used properly.

(c) 1 Tim. i. 18–20

Here (later in the same chapter) Paul repeats his insistence on the necessity of preserving a good conscience, as an indispensable prerequisite of continuing soundness in the faith. He instances by name two individuals, the tragedy of whose spiritual career provided concrete evidence and warning of the fact that no man can disregard the demands of conscience and still continue true to the Christian faith. For these men, by their deliberate indifference to moral standards —they '*put away*' or '*thrust from them*' (R.V.) a good conscience —involved their course as Christian believers in disaster; they '*made shipwreck concerning the faith*' (R.V.). For no man can thus disregard the witness of conscience and still hold to a safe course in the truth. 'A true belief will not long survive unfaithfulness to God's inward voice' (H. P. Liddon).

Some years ago the present writer had occasionally to travel by small river boat in West China. Here there are often stretches of rapid water, difficult and dangerous to navigate. The foreign traveller trusts himself to the acquired knowledge and skill of his Chinese boatmen. They surprise him at first, on going down stream in the rapids, by their energetic determination to make the boat go faster still. As rapid water is approached all available hands take to the oars and paddle hard, as if progress depended on their efforts; and in one very practical sense it does, and not only progress but also safety. For, if the many rocks and boulders are to be avoided in the swift moving water, and the boat saved from shipwreck, she must be effectively steered. But no boat will respond to her rudder unless she is moving in relation to the water in which she is to be steered. To yield to the fascinating delusion that the swift moving water is surely carrying them forward fast enough, without the need of additional effort on their part, would only involve the boatmen in certain disaster. For, at the crucial moment, the boat would not respond to the steersman. The very current that is carrying them forward would then only bring about their damage and possible destruction by dashing the boat on to the rocks.

So faith in the current is not sufficient; indeed, by itself it may be perilously misleading. There must be determined and energetic attention to the task and responsibility of steering to the right hand or to the left. Those who neglect this duty will be carried forward not to their desired destination but to their doom. Similarly, those who know how much all true spiritual progress depends upon faith in the movement towards them in grace of the living God cannot afford to forget that, if they would continue to enjoy the benefits of God-given life and salvation, they must have their senses exercised to discern between good and evil; and they must by alert and energetic devotion to the task hold fast to a good conscience.

We may remember here with profit how our Lord answered the devil's second temptation. When He was invited to throw Himself down from a pinnacle of the temple, and to trust in God and His promises of preservation, it was His conscience rather than His faith that answered: 'But that would be wrong. For it is also written, "*Thou shalt not tempt the Lord thy God*"' (Mt. iv. 5–7).

(*d*) *Pr. xvi.* 6

'*By the fear of the Lord men depart from evil.*' According to the Old Testament Scriptures the first principle of life to be taught to children is active reverence for the living God. '*The fear of the Lord is the beginning of wisdom*' (Ps. cxi. 10). In other words, proper reverence for God is the indispensable foundation of all right understanding. Only in God's light can we see. (See Ps. xxxvi. 9.) The same principle is expressed in the New Testament by statements such as '*Godliness is profitable unto all things*' (1 Tim. iv. 8); '*For we walk by faith, not by sight*' (2 Cor. v. 7); '*Through faith we understand . . .*' (Heb. xi. 3). According to the same Old Testament Scriptures the next thing to be taught to the growing child is moral discernment. The child must learn in the fear of God '*to refuse the evil, and choose the good*' (Is. vii. 15, 16). Similarly, the sign of Christian growth to maturity is '*by reason of use*' to have one's '*senses exercised to discern both good and evil*' (Heb. v. 14). It is only by the combination of these two activities of reverence for God and moral discrimination that life can be rightly directed; for to avoid shipwreck one must hold both faith and a good conscience.

(*e*) *Ps. cxix. 11*

'*Thy word have I hid in mine heart, that I might not sin against thee.*' The believer in God is clearly meant thus to grow in powers of moral discernment by his increasing knowledge of the Word of God, and his growing ability to apply it. The

Bible abounds in plain instructions concerning personal behaviour; it indicates the principles which should govern conduct. In many matters in life the Bible leaves us in no doubt which way is right and which way is wrong. It is according to one's measure of knowledge that conscience can and ought to function to approve or disapprove, to constrain or restrain. '*To him that knoweth to do good, and doeth it not, to him it is sin*' (Jas. iv. 17). Such obligations governing right conduct operate in relation first to God, then to others, and finally to oneself. They embrace and concern every activity and relationship of human life. Only those can and do fully obey God's Word and enjoy its promised blessings, who make it their diligent and unceasing concern to be well-pleasing to the Lord in everything they do. So there is need for each one of us so to live that he can say, as Paul said of himself, '*And herein do I exercise myself, to have always a conscience void of offence toward God, and toward men*' (Acts xxiv. 16).

CHAPTER VIII

THE PRACTICE OF OBEDIENCE (2)

THE gospel of God's saving grace demands, as we have seen, our obedience to the life-giving Lord, if we are to enjoy its benefits and His salvation. Obedience to the truth of the gospel does not, however, end there. Those who thus enter into the sphere of its blessing find themselves by God's appointment inevitably involved in a twofold stewardship. It becomes their privilege and responsibility on the one hand to propagate to others, and on the other hand to preserve whole and entire, the very Word of God's saving grace to which they owe their salvation, and their consequent membership in the people of God. It is these two responsibilities which we are now to consider.

I. PROPAGATING THE GOSPEL

If, as true disciples or devoted followers of Christ, we are to become fully obedient to His Word, there is one plain imperative demand of His whose challenge we must face, and that is the demand to make Him known as the Saviour of men. For the risen Lord explicitly commissioned His followers to proclaim to all men the gospel of His Person and His work. So we cannot be fully obedient to His Word unless we take our share in the discharge of this commission.

(*a*) *Mt. xxviii. 19, 20; Mk. xvi. 15; Lk. xxiv. 44–48; Jn. xx. 21–23*

Each one of the four Gospel records includes as it closes explicit mention of this missionary commission. So we read in Mt. xxviii. 19, 20: '*Go ye therefore, and teach all nations, baptizing them in the name of the Father, and of the Son, and of the Holy Ghost: teaching them to observe all things whatsoever I have commanded you.*' Likewise in Mk. xvi. 15: '*Go ye into all the world, and preach the gospel to every creature.*'

In Lk. xxiv. 44–48 there is a significant explanatory statement. We are told that the risen Lord showed clearly to His disciples from the Scriptures that His suffering and His resurrection were both fulfilments of what the Scriptures foretold, and that they accomplished God's foreordained purpose. It was therefore nothing less than necessary that He should so suffer and rise again. Now, He asserted, because this necessary work has been accomplished, there is, as the prophecies of the Old Testament had foreshadowed, a gospel to be preached—a gospel of salvation from sin, the benefits of which can be freely offered to the whole world. Now, He said, God intends '*that repentance and remission of sins should be preached in his name among all nations.*' Also, He said, that the place to begin the preaching is '*at Jerusalem*'; in other words, the gospel is to be preached to the Jews first, and then to the Gentiles. '*And*', He added, '*ye are witnesses of these things*'; or, as we might say, 'you are the people to do the preaching.'

In effect Jesus said: I have done the indispensable work of redemption and reconciliation. You are to do the complementary work of proclamation and exhortation, offering men salvation through Christ's finished work, and beseeching them thus to make their peace with God. Here then we have the divine authority, the scriptural sanction, and the Master's own charter for world-wide Christian missionary effort, and for our place in it as Christ's witnesses. For it is God's eternal purpose thus to provide salvation in Christ; to this the Old Testament bears witness. This purpose has been fulfilled; Christ has died for our sins, and He is risen and all-powerful to save; so present salvation is available. But men will enjoy this benefit, only if news of it is proclaimed. This proclamation is a task committed by Christ to His followers. Those who become believers in Christ and disciples of Christ are then meant by God's appointment and Christ's command to take some share in winning others to become His disciples.

The words recorded in Jn. xx. 21–23 indicate, if possible still more profoundly, the direct divine sanction and the solemn eternal character of such service. For Christ's commission to His disciples thus to preach salvation to the world is similar and complementary to His own commission as the Son of God to be the Saviour of the world. This Christ made plain when He said, '*As my Father hath sent me, even so send I you.*' Not only so: He went on to indicate that those who engage in this ministry are to be empowered for it by the God-given Spirit, and will thus share in a task which settles for ever men's eternal destiny. For, if the preacher of this gospel offers a sinner salvation in Christ's name, and the sinner believes in the Saviour, then that sinner finds eternal forgiveness. His sins will never again be charged against him. So, said the Master to His commissioned preachers, '*Whose soever sins ye remit, they are remitted unto them.*' In other words, to lead men in repentance and faith to obey the gospel and to trust in the Saviour is to do work of eternal moment, whose results will abide for ever. Similarly, and even more solemnly, when any hear the gospel from human preachers and reject it, they involve themselves in eternal condemnation. Their sins return upon their own heads, and there irremovably remain. So, said the Master to His commissioned preachers, '*and whose soever sins ye retain, they are retained*'. What is more, Christ thus spoke not to the eleven only but to a general gathering of disciples. These words, therefore, are not words authorizing a formal priestly absolution to be given only by some select and privileged hierarchy. They are rather words indicating the divine and eternal character of the commission to evangelize, which rests upon all Christ's followers.

(*b*) *Mt. xiv. 15–21, xv. 21–28, 32–38*

Now that we know what was the goal in view we may profitably look earlier and see how these ideas were anticipated in our Lord's teaching of the disciples. By some of the things which He did with them, or allowed them to do with Him, during His earthly ministry, our Lord was preparing their minds, in ways which they did not appreciate at the time, for the full task of the future. Let us consider, for instance, the familiar stories of the feeding of the multitudes. Here on two different occasions we find Christ working a miracle to provide supplies, and then using the disciples to get the supplies distributed. He was the indispensable Master workman; yet He deliberately made them into necessary fellow-workers. The one source from which the supplies all came was Himself. The loaves became more than enough for all when He broke them. But although His hand alone could thus break the bread, it was His chosen method that the broken pieces should reach the needy not by His hand but by the hands of the disciples. So He '*gave . . . to his disciples, and the disciples to the multitude*'. Thus in the simplest form is illustrated the staggering truth that once we know Him and become His followers, we stand between His saving grace and a needy world, as those who are entrusted with the privilege and responsibility of carrying to men the knowledge of the saving grace of Christ. So, when we would '*send the multitude away*', He says, '*They need not depart; give ye them to eat.*'

Also, while the first feeding was of a Jewish multitude, there is evidence for supposing that the second feeding was of a Gentile multitude. For it is recorded of them, as though they themselves were not Israelites, that '*they glorified the God of Israel*' (Mt. xv. 31). And between the two stories comes the story of the Syro-Phoenician woman, who was a Gentile. She came beseeching Christ to have mercy on her. Before He met her need, He raised the question, 'Is it right *to take the children's bread, and to cast it to dogs?*' In other words, it was as if He were asking, 'If God provides bread for His children, to whom should it be given? to Jews only? or also to people of other nations?' Then He answered both the request of the woman and His own question by ministering to her need, not because she was a Jew, but because she was a believer. He said unto her, '*O woman, great is thy faith: be it unto thee even as thou wilt.*' Thus He 'gave bread' to a Gentile believer. Similarly, shortly afterwards He gave actual bread to the Gentile multitude. Surely He was thus teaching His disciples that the salvation which He had come into the world to provide was for the Jews of course, but also for the world; indeed, in the feeding of the second multitude He actually used them in ministry to feed Gentiles. So were their minds prepared to appreciate later that the gospel with which He entrusted them was to be preached '*to the Jew first, and also to the Greek*' (Rom. i. 16), and that it was their business and responsibility to preach it. This is still the responsibility of all true disciples of Christ, to see that the spiritually hungry are given the Bread of Life.

(c) 2 Cor. v. 18–20

If we turn on into the Epistles we find the same ideas endorsed by the witness of the apostles. In particular let us notice how the apostle Paul was made to share in the same awareness and the same convictions. In 2 Cor. v. 18–20 he declares that God has done two complementary things. He has '*reconciled us to himself by Jesus Christ*'; and He has '*given to us the ministry of reconciliation*'. He entrusted to Christ the work of reconciliation, He has '*committed unto us the word of reconciliation*'. On the tree Christ took our place as sinners and bore sin's condemnation. Now we are to take His place in the mission field of the world, and to beseech men in His stead to accept God's terms of peace, and to be reconciled to God. Such gospel witness, such missionary work, is nothing less than a complementary part of God's purpose for the redemption of men and their reconciliation to Himself, complementary that is to the work of Christ's own death for our sins. These two activities belong together, the finished work of Christ on the cross and the continued witness in the world of His ambassadors. Just as Christ had of divine necessity to suffer and to rise again, so must '*this gospel . . . be preached in all the world for a witness unto all nations*'; only '*then shall the end come*'. (See Mt. xxiv. 14; Mk. xiii. 10.) There is, therefore, no more glorious task, no higher vocation, no better obedience, than to publish to needy sinners heaven's good news of salvation and thus to become a fellow-worker with God and a partner in the business of the Master, the Master who said—and still says—'*Follow me, and I will make you fishers of men.*' (Mt. iv. 19.)

II. PRESERVING THE WITNESS

If the truth of the gospel is thus to be faithfully preached and propagated in the world, it must first of all be diligently preserved in purity and completeness without addition or diminution by those who hold it in trust; and also faithfully handed on intact both to new adherents to the faith, and to the rising generation. Only so will the regions beyond and the children yet unborn receive in its fulness the God-given truths without loss or perversion.

(*a*) *1 Tim. vi. 20; 2 Tim. ii. 2*

In the New Testament Epistles workers for God are solemnly charged first to guard the deposit of truth—to keep that which is committed to their trust—and then carefully to hand it on to others, who in their turn will do the same. So Paul wrote to Timothy: '*Keep that which is committed to thy trust*'; and later, '*And the things that thou hast heard of me among many witnesses, the same commit thou to faithful men, who shall be able to teach others also.*'

The ideas underlying these exhortations are covered in Article xx of the Thirty-Nine Articles of the Church of England by the statement that the Church is 'a witness and a keeper of holy Writ'. The emphasis here on the written form of God's Word is important. For the expression of the gospel and of the teaching of our Lord, which we have in the apostolic writings of the New Testament, has given them a permanent fixed form of known limits, sometimes called the Canon of Scripture. And it is the calling and the responsibility of God's people to preserve and to proclaim the witness of this inspired Word of God by guarding it in its entirety, as something God-given for our learning, and by testifying to its authority by using it as the determinative rule of faith and practice and the decisive text-book of all preaching and teaching.

(*b*) *Gal. ii. 1–16*

All Christians share to some extent in this stewardship of the God-given Word and in the responsibility to maintain unimpaired the apostolic succession of witness to the truth. This responsibility obviously rests particularly and most directly on those called of God to the public ministry of His Word in preaching and teaching. So Paul wrote of himself and of others like him such as Apollos or Peter: '*Let a man so account of us, as of the ministers of Christ, and stewards of the mysteries of God. Moreover it is required in stewards, that a man be found faithful'* (1 Cor. iv. 1, 2).

This faithful preservation of the witness ought to be maintained, not just in defensive self-preservation or mere negative protestantism, but rather in a spirit of positive self-sacrificing devotion to the continuance of the witness and work of the gospel of God in the world. In other words, it ought to be done, and it needs to be done, in the interest of the salvation of the lost; in the interest, that is, of giving to men and preserving for the future—for the world, for our children, and indeed for ourselves—the full and true gospel of salvation.

What the discharge of this responsibility may involve, and why such action may be necessary, are shown very clearly in the Epistle to the Galatians. Here we find genuine converts to faith in Christ and the gospel of saving grace being perverted through being taught things radically different. Here we find Paul, back from the mission field, in the home church of Jerusalem itself, having to resist pressure (to have Titus circumcised) that he saw would deprive converts in the churches of Galatia of their liberty in Christ and bring them under the bondage of legalism and ceremonialism. Here we find Paul at Antioch having publicly to withstand even Peter to the face, because, in changing his behaviour as a Christian, Peter ceased to walk uprightly according to the truth of the gospel. Paul did this because he saw clearly what was at stake; '*that the truth of the gospel*', as he puts it, '*might continue with you*' (i.e., you Galatians or mission-field converts). He stood firm and made his protest because he saw that to yield on such a point would be to betray Christian liberty, gospel truth and Gentile evangelism. How important it is, therefore, that in our own day—a day of fresh missionary expansion—we should still recognize that, if full loyalty to the truth of the gospel is not preserved in the home churches by unyielding steadfastness and by possible necessary protest even in high places, the same truth of the gospel will soon no longer be preached and practised in its full purity and entirety in the churches of the mission fields. There is still need, therefore, for faithful stewards of the God-given Word to '*contend earnestly for the faith which was once for all delivered unto the saints*' (Jude 3, R.V.), and to oppose the subtle or specious introduction of doctrines and practices, which involve nothing less than a return to legalism, a denial of salvation only by grace and through faith, and a departure from the pathway of true loyalty to the very gospel of God.

(c) 2 Tim. i. 12–14

In this connection it is important to remember that, because soundness in the faith is not a matter merely of theoretical correctness of ideas but rather concerns one's vital spiritual well-being in the life of true discipleship, there are inevitable moral conditions of continuing in spiritual health. This is a truth of which we have already taken notice when considering the need to preserve a good conscience. The same truth is enforced here by Paul's words to Timothy. Those who would '*hold fast the form of sound words*' must do so '*in faith and love which is in Christ Jesus*'. For unless true Christian faith and love are vitally active in one's life one cannot properly share in preserving the witness for the truth of the gospel.

Finally, in this task of preserving the witness, we can always count upon the unfailing help of God Himself. A possible rendering of the Greek of 2 Tim. i. 12 justifies the translation provided in the R.V. margin: '*For I know him whom I have believed, and I am persuaded that he is able to guard that which he hath committed unto me*' (Greek, 'my deposit', compare 1 Tim. vi. 20 and 2 Tim. i. 14, R.V. margin). In this same context Paul also reminds Timothy that the Holy Spirit is given to dwell in the people of God for this very purpose—to preserve the witness. (Cf. Acts i. 8.) God Himself can therefore be counted on to guard His own truth. He will not leave Himself without witness. And as those to whom He has thus given His Spirit we are called to be fellow-workers with God and with one another in this task of '*striving together for the faith of the gospel*' (Phil. i. 27).

CHAPTER IX

THE ULTIMATE ISSUES

OBEYING God's Word is of supreme importance because of its certain consequences or crowning rewards. God's Word is never an end in itself. It always has an end in view. God's speaking is always complemented by His doing. So we read: '*For he spake, and it was done*' (Ps. xxxiii. 9); and '*Hath he said, and shall he not do it?*' (Nu. xxiii. 19). Similarly man's reaction and response to the Word of God, whether in obedience or disobedience, must inevitably issue in some corresponding fulfilment, some outworked result. It is a distinctive characteristic of the inspired Word of God to make unmistakably plain what these ultimate issues are, and to challenge men to let their present activity be determined wholly in the light of them. It is equally characteristic of the inspired Word of God that it distinguishes clearly two, and only two, alternatives, the pathway of obedience and the pathway of disobedience, leading to their inevitable and completely different ends, ends as different in essential character as light and darkness, life and death. Let us, therefore, make it our concern in this last chapter to consider these alternatives and their ultimate issues.

I. THE ALTERNATIVES

The only alternative to obedience is disobedience. But those who fall into it are rarely aware of the true character and gravity of their action. For it begins in a less assertive form as simply a failure to do what God has commanded; and the very person who does this may be blinded to the seriousness of such failure by the satisfaction he finds in having heard God's Word, and in apparently knowing all about it. He is thus able to make a profession of discipleship, and to answer all the questions; but he is not a doer.

(*a*) *Mt. vii. 21–27*

At the end of the Sermon on the Mount, after our Lord had given His professed disciples much teaching, to which they had all listened, He spoke in abrupt and graphic warning of the folly of the failure to do, as something which, when the real test comes, must end in inevitable disaster. What are, in a very significant sense, the last words on this subject are these words with which our Lord Himself thus finished His teaching. We do well to note them. '*Not every one that saith unto me, Lord, Lord, shall enter into the kingdom of heaven; but he that doeth the will of my Father which is in heaven. . . . And every one that heareth these sayings of mine, and doeth them not, shall be likened unto a foolish man, which built his house upon the sand: And the rain descended, and the floods came, and the winds blew, and beat upon that house; and it fell: and great was the fall of it.*'

(*b*) *Jn. viii. 31–34*

Our Lord made practical adherence to His teaching and sustained observance of His commands an indispensable condition of true discipleship, the condition both of knowing the truth and of finding in its knowledge true freedom. He went on to state with equal clarity and dogmatic brevity the only alternative. To human reckoning there may seem many roads to choose between, other than the one narrow road of devotion to the Master's Word. But Christ embraced all such possible roads under the one description of sinning or missing the mark. For they all involve failure to do the right, and the inevitable consequence of failure to reach the true goal of human existence—the glorious liberty of the children of God. Not only so, they all involve not only the ultimate consequence, but also the immediate result here and now, of bondage. For, as Jesus said, with emphatic solemnity, '*Every one that committeth sin is the bondservant of sin*' (R.V.). So the only alternative to God-given freedom is a condition of sin-wrought slavery.

(*c*) *2 Thes. ii. 7–12*

In the final outworking of disobedience, when all restraint is removed, the spirit of opposition to God must find its full manifestation. Then, so we are here plainly warned, those who have '*received not the love of the truth, that they might be saved*', will become deceived followers of the only alternative, 'the lie', the devil's counterfeit. This God will deliberately allow for their judgment. Thus will their eternal condemnation as sinners be confirmed, because they '*believed not the truth, but had pleasure in unrighteousness*'. So the only alternative to following the truth is believing the lie. (Cf. 1 Jn. i. 6.)

(*d*) *Rev. xxii. 14, 15*

Those who read them will see that these words speak for themselves. They are among the last in the whole Bible. They provide a brief, significant, final description of two types of character and of two corresponding destinies. '*They that do his commandments . . . have right to the tree of life, and may enter in through the gates into the city.*' '*Without are . . . whosoever loveth and maketh a lie.*' These are the only ultimate alternatives. It is between them that we all must make our choice.

II. THE PERIL OF DISOBEDIENCE

Disobedience is an ever-present danger, capable of involving men in eternal damage. All of us alike need to pay heed to the repeated witness and the solemn warnings of the Scriptures. It was by disobedience that the human race first fell into sin and came under God's condemnation. (See Rom. v. 19a.) It was because of disobedience that the people of Israel in Old Testament times repeatedly came under divine discipline and judgment. For instance, of the days of the Judges, we read: '*And an angel of the Lord came up from Gilgal to Bochim, and said, I made you to go up out of Egypt, and have brought you unto the land which I sware unto your fathers; and I said, I will never break my covenant with you. And ye shall make no league with the inhabitants of this land; ye shall throw down their altars: but ye have not obeyed my voice: why have ye done this? Wherefore I also said, I will not drive them out from before you; but they shall be as thorns in your sides, and their gods shall be a snare unto you*' (Jdg. ii. 1–3).

Similarly, in Samuel's day, we find the prophet solemnly warning the people: '*If ye will fear the Lord, and serve him, and obey his voice, and not rebel against the commandment of the Lord, then shall both ye and also the king that reigneth over you continue following the Lord your God: But if ye will not obey the voice of the Lord, but rebel against the commandment of the Lord, then shall the hand of the Lord be against you, as it was against your fathers*' (1 Sa. xii. 14, 15). Also, we find Samuel declaring to King Saul: '*Because thou hast rejected the word of the Lord, he hath also rejected thee from being king*' (1 Sa. xv. 23).

Later still, at the time of the separation of the kingdom of Israel from the kingdom of Judah, we learn that God said, '*Behold, I will rend the kingdom out of the hand of Solomon . . . because that they have forsaken me, . . . and have not walked in my ways.*' (1 Ki. xi. 31, 33.) Also, much later again, when even Jerusalem was destroyed, and the house of God burnt, and the people carried captive to Babylon, the chronicler summarizes the cause, by saying: '*And the Lord God of their fathers sent to them by his messengers, rising up betimes, and sending; because he had compassion on his people, and on his dwelling place: But they mocked the messengers of God, and despised his words, and misused his prophets, until the wrath of the Lord arose against his people, till there was no remedy. Therefore he brought upon them the king of the Chaldees, . . . he gave them all into his hand*' (2 Ch. xxxvi. 15–17).

When we turn to the New Testament Scriptures we find that these happenings of Old Testament times are but 'figures of the true' and shadows and types of the final realities. There is now a greater Word from God, given to men in Christ, disobedience to which will involve men in eternal judgment. '*Therefore we ought to give the more earnest heed to the things which we have heard, lest at any time we should let them slip. For if the word spoken by angels was stedfast, and every transgression and disobedience received a just recompense of reward; How shall we escape, if we neglect so great salvation; which at the first began to be spoken by the Lord, and was confirmed unto us by them that heard him?*' (Heb. ii. 1–3). For the day is coming '*when the Lord Jesus shall be revealed from heaven with his mighty angels in flaming fire*'; and then He will act in judgment as one '*taking vengeance on them that know not God, and that obey not the gospel of our Lord Jesus Christ: who shall be punished with everlasting destruction from the presence of the Lord*' (2 Thes. i. 7–9).

III. THE CROWNING REWARDS OF OBEDIENCE

If disobedience to the Word of God must thus be followed by inevitable judgment, the consequences of obedience to God's Word are equally certain and surpassingly wonderful. Of these, the crowning reward is nothing less than to become like to God Himself, and thus able to enjoy fellowship with

Him. It is, indeed, to realize 'the chief end of man', which is 'to glorify God and to enjoy Him for ever'.

(*a*) *Jn. xiv. 15, 21–24, xv. 14*

Obedience to God's Word is first of all the proper and only adequate sign of true love of God and of His Son, Jesus Christ, our Lord. So our Lord said explicitly and repeatedly, '*If ye love me, keep my commandments.*' '*He that hath my commandments, and keepeth them, he it is that loveth me.*' '*If a man love me, he will keep my words.*' '*Ye are my friends, if ye do whatsoever I command you.*' So the first reward of obedience to His commandments is that, by it, we show our love to Him who first loved us.

(*b*) *Jn. xiv. 21, 23; 1 Jn. ii. 3, 4, iii. 24*

Such obedience to God's Word leads in the second place to a significant consequence. Through it we are called to enter into a deepening knowledge of God Himself, a realized fellowship with the Father, through the Son, and by the Spirit. So our Lord said of the man, who by his obedience to His commandments shows his love to God, that '*he that loveth me shall be loved of my Father, and I will love him, and will manifest myself to him.*' And again, '*my Father will love him, and we will come unto him, and make our abode with him.*'

Consequently, when in his first Epistle John deals with the practical tests of vital Christian experience, he writes: '*And hereby we do know that we know him, if we keep his commandments. He that saith, I know him, and keepeth not his commandments, is a liar, and the truth is not in him.*' '*And he that keepeth his commandments dwelleth in him, and he in him.*'

So the second reward of obedience to His commandments is that, through it, we come to know God in intimate personal communion. For only the obedient can thus 'enjoy Him for ever'.